Also by John Callahan

Don't Worry, He Won't Get Far on Foot:
The Autobiography of a Dangerous Man

Do Not Disturb Any Further

Digesting the Child Within

Do What He Says! He's Crazy!!!

I Think I Was an Alcoholic

The Night, They Say, Was Made for Love
plus My Sexual Scrapbook

JOHN CALLAHAN

QUILL
WILLIAM MORROW
NEW YORK

It is the policy of William Morrow and Company, Inc., and its imprints and affiliates, recognizing the importance of preserving what has been written, to print the books we publish on acid-free paper, and we exert our best efforts to that end.

Library of Congress Catalog Data

Callahan, John.
    What kind of a God would allow a thing like this to happen? ! ! / by John Callahan.
        p.   cm.
    ISBN 0-688-13337-1
    1. American wit and humor, Pictorial.   I. Title.
    NC1429.C23A4   1994
    741.5'973—dc20   94-11351
                                                                CIP

Printed in the United States of America

        3   4   5   6   7   8   9   10

Acknowledgments

I'd like to thank the following people for their unending help and support: Richard Callahan, Deborah Levin, Peter Nelson, Dale Mills, Richard Pine, and especially my editor, Liza Dawson.

For David Milholland

"Hey! It's printed on recycled paper!!"

CALLAHAN

"By the way, what's the appropriate greeting here?"

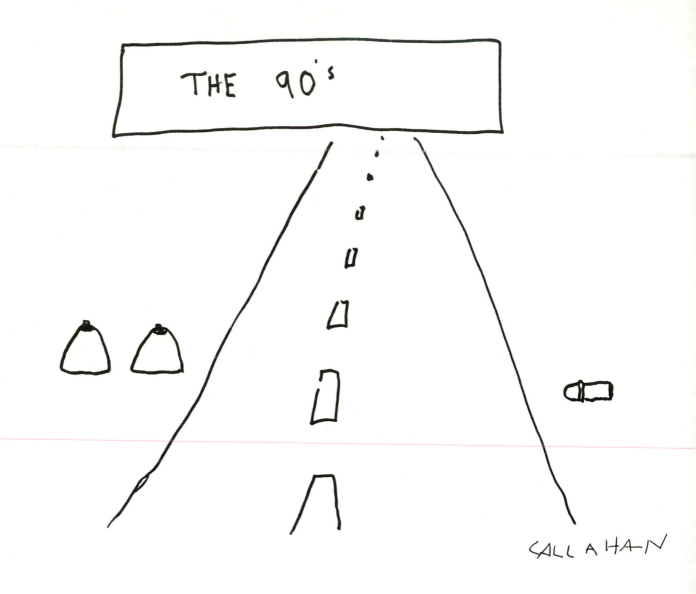

TONYA HARDING
AND
CONNIE CHUNG
ATTEMPT A
TRIPLE AXEL
IN THE 1994
WINTER OLYMPICS.

CALLAHAN

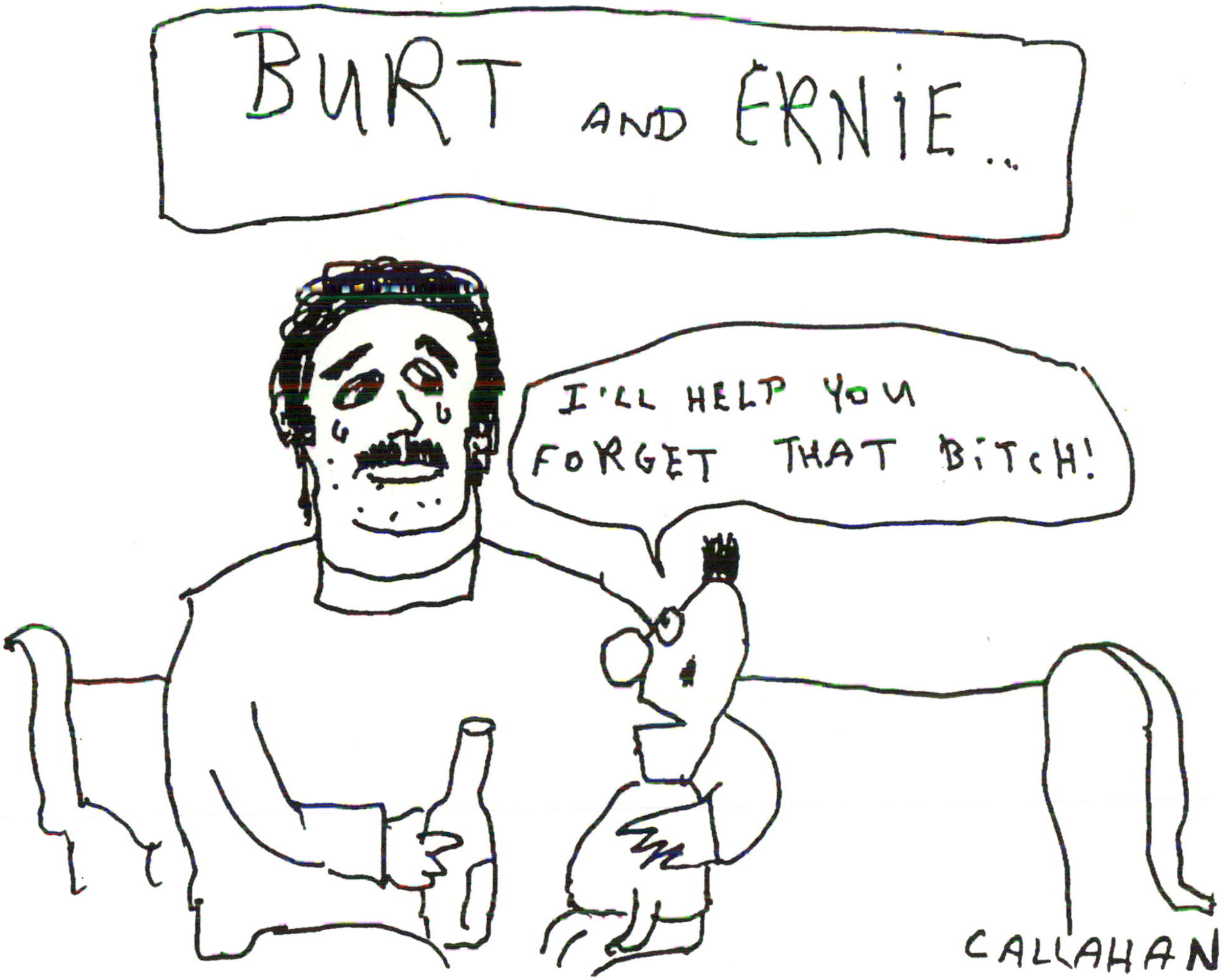
BURT AND ERNIE..
I'LL HELP YOU FORGET THAT BITCH!
CALLAHAN

THE
RUSH LIMBAUGH
MONUMENT

CALLAHAN

"Let's wok the dog."

WHY, Julie! WHAT'S THE MATTER?!
SOMEONE PINCHED MY BOTTOM BY THE WATER-COOLER! Sob! AND NOW I'M REALLY UPSET! Sob! AND I'M SUPPOSED TO BE DOWNTOWN TO SIGN UP FOR SOMETHING!!
SIGN UP FOR WHAT?!!
THE ARMY!!
CALLAHAN

CALLAHAN

"Carol . . . just how serious is your yeast infection getting?!!"

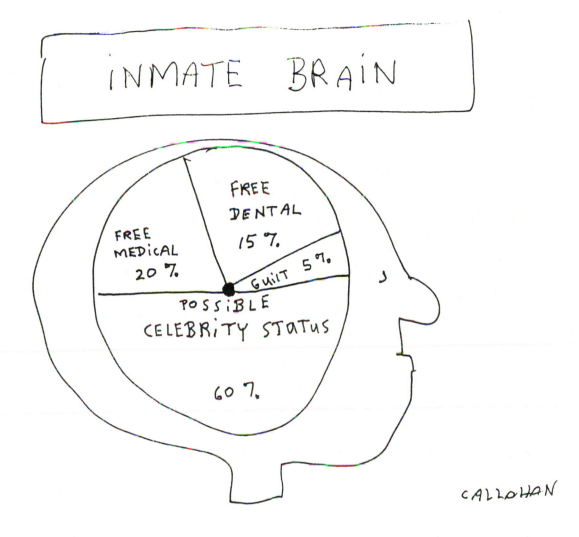

THE DIFFERENCE BETWEEN BILL CLINTON AND GEORGE BUSH.

CALLAHAN

MICHAEL FAY
"PADDLED ON
HIS BOTTOM"

CALLAHAN

43

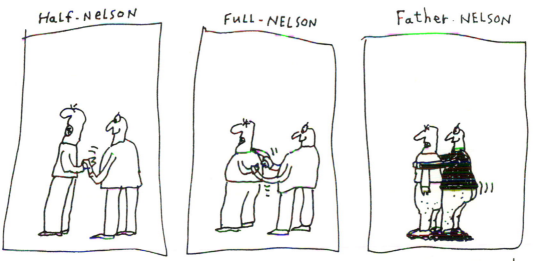

45

"May I have your permission to put my arm around you,
let my hand drop casually upon your breast, become increasingly aroused,
yet painfully conscious of my chronic inability to satisfy a woman,
and then kill you with a brick in my humiliation?"

"It's good to spend a night under the stars!"

CALLAHAN

RICHARD SIMMONS IS BEATEN UNMERCIFULLY BY A GROUP OF PEOPLE WHO LIKE BEING FAT, AND DON'T WANT TO SWEAT TO THE OLDIES.

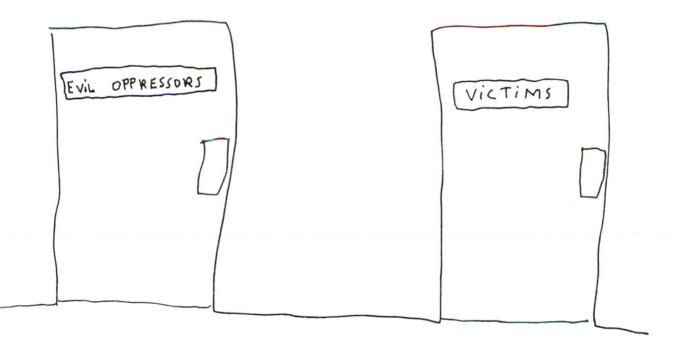

CALLAHAN

TIME: 10:23
TEMP: 90°___
RODNEY
KING
ARRESTS: 8011

CALLAHAN

"Miss Valentine, please bring me anything!"

CALLAHAN

"Space travelers hell!
We're just looking for a place to have a cigarette!!"

CALLAHAN

A MOVER AND A SHAKER

CALLAHAN

CALLAHAN

Remember... it's only sexual harassment if they're not dateable!
CALLAHAN

"She's a bit heavy, but she's got lovely personalities."

CELEBRITY
FUGITIVE
LANE

CALLAHAN

WEST SIDE BULIMIA CLINIC

HAPPY HALLOWEEN

CALLAHAN

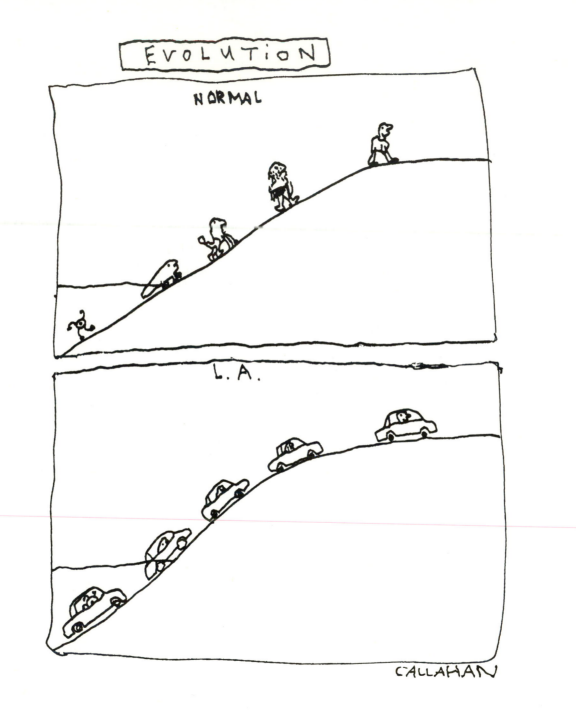

93

IN THE NEWS, ON THIS 24th OF DECEMBER... ...MINORITIES ARE GENETICALLY INFERIOR... WOMEN ARE USELESS... ABORTION IS IMMORAL... NATURAL RESOURCES ARE EXPENDABLE... AND VIOLENT CRIMINALS ARE NOT SAINTS! ...JUST KIDDING!
CALLAHAN
A P.C. NIGHTMARE BEFORE CHRISTMAS

"Madonna!! Where are you!!!"

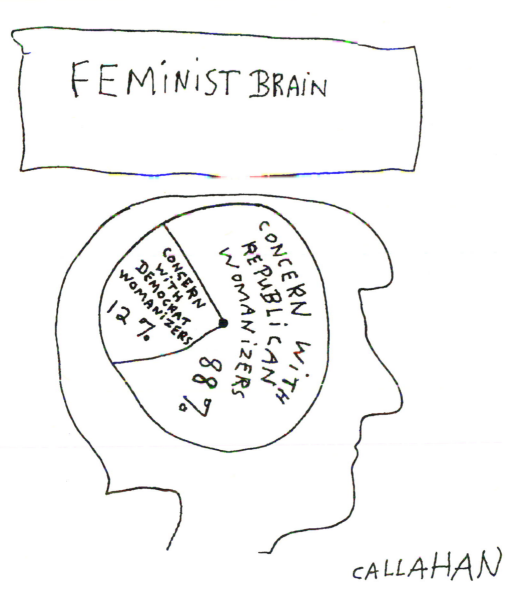

NOW, WHEN WE GET TO THE TOP LET'S SAY WE'RE CHRISTIANS AND DENY THE WHOLE THING HAPPENED!
CALLAHAN

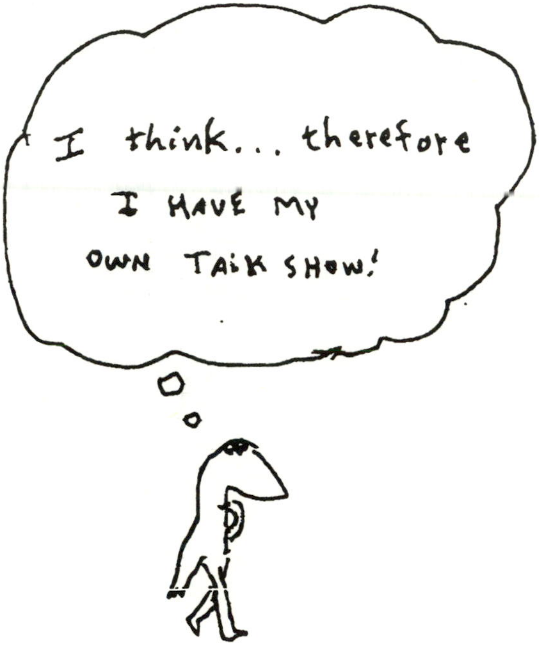

CALLAHAN